THE YOUNG
INDIANA JONES
CHRONICLES™
ON THE SET AND BEHIND THE SCENES

THE YOUNG INDIANA JONES CHRONICLES™

ON THE SET AND BEHIND THE SCENES

DAN MADSEN

BANTAM BOOKS
NEW YORK · TORONTO · LONDON · SYDNEY · AUCKLAND

RL 6, age 10 and up

THE YOUNG INDIANA JONES CHRONICLES™
A Bantam Book / April 1992

*The Young Indiana Jones Chronicles
is a trademark of Lucasfilm Ltd.*

ISBN 0-553-37006-5

Published simultaneously in the United States and Canada

*Bantam Books are published by Bantam Books, a division of
Bantam Doubleday Dell Publishing Group, Inc. Its trademark,
consisting of the words "Bantam Books" and the portrayal of a
rooster, is Registered in U.S. Patent and Trademark Office and in
other countries. Marca Registrada. Bantam Books, 666 Fifth
Avenue, New York, New York 10103.*

PRINTED IN THE UNITED STATES OF AMERICA

CWO   0 9 8 7 6 5 4 3 2 1

Contents

Introduction

Have you ever dreamed of traveling all over the world? Climbing the Great Pyramid of Giza, walking the halls of the Taj Mahal in India or through the ancient ruins of the Acropolis in Greece? Maybe you've imagined what it must be like to be the first person to uncover an ancient tomb or to find an ancient relic from a lost civilization. Perhaps you've even wondered what it would be like to meet some of the greatest minds of the twentieth century face-to-face—the very people who shaped the history of the world.

Most of us only dream of such experiences. But for one street-smart New Jersey kid, these experiences are merely pages from the book of his life. We're speaking, of course, about that intrepid explorer Henry Jones, Jr.—known better to all of us as Indiana Jones.

The excitement and adventure of one of the most unconventional childhoods imaginable is now the subject of a new, weekly television series from George Lucas called *The Young Indiana Jones Chronicles*. Each episode takes viewers on a journey with Indy as he travels all over the world. Whether he's eight years old and accompanying his mother and father on a worldwide lecture tour or a young man of eighteen fighting during World War I, *The Young Indiana Jones Chronicles* focuses on the coming-of-age of one of the most beloved heroes ever created in film history.

In the eleven years since his introduction in the blockbuster film *Raiders of the Lost Ark,* Indiana Jones has become a legendary hero embraced by millions around the world. He is a character of incredible dimension: dashing, independent, scholarly, yet physical, adventurous, and committed to truth and fair play among men and nations. Indy's appeal is universal, and for a decade he has had movie audiences eagerly awaiting each new film.

The idea for the Indiana Jones films first came to George Lucas in the early 1970s. He wanted to make a movie that harkened back to the days of the 1930s cliffhanger serials. So, in 1977, shortly after *Star Wars* had opened, George Lucas took a vacation in Hawaii with friend Steven Spielberg. Sitting on the beach one sunny afternoon, he told his filmmaking colleague about a character he had created—an archaeologist/adventurer on a heroic mission to save the Lost Ark of the Covenant from the sinister clutches of Hitler. Shortly thereafter, in June of 1980, the two filmmakers set out to make *Raiders of the Lost Ark*.

With actor Harrison Ford playing the part of Indiana Jones, the character's popularity grew with each film. All three of the Indiana Jones films rank among the top-ten box-office hits of all time. Moviegoers were drawn, in record-breaking numbers, to see each cliffhanging, hair-raising adventure. But even with all the heroics Indy exhibited, actor Harrison Ford never saw Indy as a true hero. The actor always envisioned the larger-than-life adventurer as "a man who stumbles into dangerous situations and is forced by his own instinct for self-preservation to act heroically.

"He's an archaeologist," Ford has said, "and at the same time an adventurer unconstrained by the usual niceties of the academic world. He is a swashbuckling type, but he has human frailties, fears, and money problems. He teaches, but I wouldn't describe him as an intellectual. He does brave things, but I wouldn't call him a hero. He's just in there with a bullwhip to keep the world at bay."

Throughout the early films it appeared as if movie-goers all wanted to know how the Indiana Jones they loved so much came to be. So in *Indiana Jones and the Last Crusade,* George Lucas whetted our appetite for the answer by casting actor River Phoenix as Young Indy. This is the film that gave rise to *The Young Indiana Jones Chronicles*—a project that Lucas has put his full efforts and attention into.

"It started out of a love of an idea," the filmmaker says, recalling the inspiration for the series. "I have an educational foundation working on interactive projects, and I got this idea to get kids involved in history through the Young Indiana Jones character. The turn of the century is my favorite part of history because it has so much to do with the emergence of the modern age we live in today. It seemed like such a great idea and such an interesting adventure that I just got lured into it by the creative potential. I took it to the network and said, 'Would you be interested in this? It's a little bit esoteric for television,' but they said, 'Great!' They've been very cooperative and we've been off making this adventure ever since . . . and it has been a true adventure."

The Young Indiana Jones Chronicles and the Indiana Jones motion pictures have much in common. They can all be described as productions of epic proportions, and they all share the same character. But it was one essential difference that sparked Lucas's initial interest—they use two completely different mediums.

"I was eager to experiment with a few production techniques that I had always wanted to incorporate in

(From left to right) Actor Sean Patrick Flanery, Executive Producer George Lucas, and Producer Rick McCallum on the set of the Congo 1917 episode.

making the features, but I've never really been in a situation where I could afford to do it," he says. "In a feature, when a mistake is made, it costs you huge amounts of money. Because *The Young Indiana Jones Chronicles* is not every expensive to produce—they're moderately priced hour adventure shows—I really wanted to see if I could successfully use feature-production techniques in the context of a TV series. So part of it was a production experiment, and part of it was trying to deal with this creative idea that's sort of esoteric. The episodes take place all over the world. We're shooting in eleven different countries. We cover everything imaginable, from the Mexican Revolution to the Russian Revolution to World War I. It's really exciting in that it has such a huge scope. It's actually bigger in scope than any of the features I've done."

One of the other unique aspects of *The Young Indiana Jones Chronicles* is the fact that we witness Young Indy's adventures at two different stages of his life. As the series begins we are introduced to Indy at age eight, and later we meet him at age sixteen. Each episode also opens and closes with the character reminiscing about those adventures at age ninety-three—something no other television series has done. But what inspired George Lucas to focus on the character at these different stages of life?

"That's something that some people weren't too happy to have me do, but I really wanted to tell about those two periods in time," the filmmaker responds. "Both are very interesting periods, and I didn't want to do one, and then if the series went well, do the other. I really wanted to deal with both periods and mix it up. . . .

"The network and the studio were afraid," Lucas continues, "because television has its rules and its little formulas that they go by. They want one strong identifiable figure. Television is a character-driven medium, so they're very focused on making sure that they basically have one marketable figure or actor. We actually have three different actors playing Indiana Jones. And there's a possibility, if it goes another year, that Indy will range from a five-year-old all the way up to a twenty-two-year-old. It's all the Indiana Jones character personified by Harrison Ford in his midthirties, but in these other time periods you can't use Harrison, so I think it's perfectly natural that different actors play those characters. The show explores how Indiana Jones got to be the way he is. How, like in the features, did he learn to speak so many languages? Where did he pick that up? How did he decide to become an archaeologist? There are so many fascinating things about the character that you can't deal with in the features because they move along so fast on an action level. I thought it would be interesting to understand how that happened and to build up, mainly for the teenage audience, a character who likes to learn. He's not a nerd; he's not a jerk, but he loves learning and what the result of that learning gets him in the end. It doesn't make him rich or famous, but it definitely puts him in good stead in terms of his walking through life."

After Lucas made the decision to go ahead with the series, he called up his longtime friends Steven Spielberg and Harrison Ford, to get their reaction. They were very supportive.

Lucas also commented that "ABC has been very supportive. I sort of enjoy the fact that I don't know that much about television. I'm just doing what I want to do. I'm creating this thing that I enjoy and conforming to the sort of standards that belong in television in terms of time and where the commercials go and those sorts of things. But I'm basically getting to tell the stories that I want to tell, and that's really what excites me about this."

As with most of his productions, Lucas is involved in every step of the Young Indy series—from the initial story conferences with the writers to the actual filming and, finally, the editing.

"The secret is hiring good people," says Lucas. "I work with the directors and get them to agree with what we want to do, and then they go out and do it. I show up periodically. Every few weeks I go out and check on everything, but the truth of it is, there's nothing you can do even if you're standing there. I mean, it's the director's medium, and he's going to do what he wants to do. I have the opportunity, when it comes back here, to have a great deal of control over how it's finished, which I think is also where quality comes into it, but I'm taking more time to finish these shows than most people spend on television. An extremely important part of quality filmmaking is the postproduction schedule, and we're spending extra time and money on the postproduction schedule to make sure it comes out right."

For George Lucas, *The Young Indiana Jones Chronicles* is the culmination of years of hard work and tedious planning. The television series allows us to understand the film character we have all come to know and love in much greater detail. These are the stories that explain how Indiana Jones came to be.

"This is the true life story of the man that the character was based on in the features," Lucas states. "It's about somebody who's very interested in learning about things, somebody who's had some incredible adventures in his life that really revolve more around learning and exploring various ideas than getting involved in action/adventure things.

"It's very time-consuming," Lucas adds. "You're doing

fifteen hours, which is the equivalent of seven movies. Normally I do one or two movies a year. Now I'm doing the equivalent of seven movies a year! It's really intense, but it's fun, too," he concludes with a smile. "I'm having a ball with the whole thing!"

1

Indy Times Three

✪ **COREY CARRIER**

As *The Young Indiana Jones Chronicles* begins, we meet up with a precocious and intuitive young man who has an insatiable curiosity about the world. He's eight-year-old Indiana Jones. The young actor portraying our favorite worldly adventurer at this age is Corey Carrier.

Carrier, who turned eleven this past year, is no stranger to acting. He has performed in such feature films as *My Blue Heaven, After Dark My Sweet, Crazy People*, and *The Witches of Eastwick*. When George Lucas and company set out to cast the role of Young Indy, they knew they would have to find a bright and talented young man who could display some of the youthful charm of the would-be archaeologist. As luck would have it, Corey Carrier got called in for an audition.

"Well, my manager got a list of the shows that you could try out for," says Carrier, "and this show came up, so I went in for it and met some people. They gave me a script. I studied it, learned it, and went in there and just said the lines. They said, 'That's good. Can you come back maybe Wednesday?' They made an appointment and I just kept coming back until I met the producer, Rick McCallum. Then, on the third or fourth try, I met George Lucas, so I guess they liked me and I was cast for the role."

Corey says he's seen all the Indiana Jones films many times and that his favorite is *Indiana Jones and the Last Crusade*. He especially liked Sean Connery's portrayal of Indy's father, Professor Henry Jones. It's ironic that when the first Indiana Jones film, *Raiders of the Lost Ark*, was made, Corey had not even been born! For Corey, some of the most fun has been doing his own stunts.

"I have tarantulas crawl all over my hands," he says with a grin. "I pick up snakes, too. As a matter of fact, tomorrow there's a kid coming over to my house who has a python, but a small thin python, and we're going to play around with it so I can get the feel of a snake in my hands."

Now, most people would shy away from snakes, including Indiana Jones himself! In *Raiders of the Lost Ark*, Indy wasn't too pleased that the Well of Souls, which he had to lower himself into in order to reach the lost Ark of the Covenant, was filled with snakes. But fortunately for Corey, it's not much of a problem.

Production of *The Young Indiana Jones Chronicles* has taken Corey to different countries all over the world for almost a year. Some might think that because of his busy work schedule, he gets to skip school. But that isn't so. Like any normal eleven-year-old, Corey has to study. Just as Young Indy has his tutor, Helen, so, too, does Corey.

"My mother is my tutor," the young actor reveals. "She's a certified schoolteacher, so she really gets all my books from the school. They send them here, and then she just teaches me. Last year, when I was in fifth grade, I got all A's for two terms. Last term, with my mother, I made 'high honors,' which is all A's, too.

"I have to spend three hours a day studying while I'm doing the series," Corey continues. "Sometimes I do more. Occasionally, we'll go on a field trip, like to an Egyptian museum or a Spanish museum."

For Corey, working on the series has been an education in itself. He's been to places that many only dream of.

"I've met a lot of cool kids that are from different places. There's this really nice kid Isaac. He knows four languages, including English. We get along well. We've been hanging out and doing stuff together. I've learned some things from him. I can now count up to ten in Maasai, so that's really cool! I know a little bit in Spanish, too. I know a bit of Chinese and, really, everywhere I've gone, I've learned at least a little bit. You know, enough to say, 'Where's that?'"

One of George Lucas's goals with *The Young Indiana Jones Chronicles* was to get young people interested in history by bringing many of the colorful stories and exciting people of the past to life. For Corey Carrier, just making the episodes has taught him a great deal about some of these events and people.

"I've learned a lot," he says. "I've learned about King Tut, I've learned about President Roosevelt, I've learned about safaris, I've learned about animals, I've learned about different cultures, and so many things that I couldn't really learn from a textbook. This is real life, so I'm going to the places where this has really happened."

While Corey's mother travels with him all over the world, she's not alone. The rest of Corey's family has also come along for the ride to see the sights and sounds of the world.

"I think my sister really likes traveling," Corey remarks. "She's getting books from everyplace. My mother and father like it, too. It's really an opportunity to do so many things."

But how do they all travel? Is it difficult?

"My mother, father, sister, and I stay in a tent or a nice hotel. Usually they're really nice hotels, with room service every night and a huge breakfast. Or we stay in tents, like down at the Mara River, in Africa, which is really great because I caught a lizard and I named him 'Indy.' So we stay in one place a month, leave, stay in one place a week, leave, go to a different part of another country . . . stuff like that."

Besides his three hours of schoolwork and his occasional time off, Corey's average day on the set is a full day's work. But he admits it doesn't seem like work since he's having so much fun.

"Usually, we work five or six days a week, but the hours are good. Most of the time we get Saturday or Sunday off. We get up around nine; sometimes we get up earlier, but that's if we've got to get a real dawn shot, a shot of the sun coming up. But other than that, the hours are really good. We get back around six or seven and I go swimming in the pool, no matter where we are."

As George Lucas has said, *The Young Indiana Jones Chronicles* is unique as far as television series go because there are two actors playing the same character at different ages. Corey's older counterpart is actor Sean Patrick Flanery—who portrays Indy at eighteen. Because they play the same character, one might think that the two actors would compare notes to help each other with their portrayal. But that isn't necessarily so.

"We only see each other once every two countries," says Corey. "And when we do see each other, we talk about personal stuff. Sometimes we talk about the scripts, but usually we talk about what bands we like or what episodes we have to do. We go to the beach or go skateboarding, things like that."

Every week a new adventure awaits Indy; new people to meet, new places to visit, new things to learn. The same is true for Corey Carrier as he films each episode in different exotic locations. Certainly many exciting things happened on the set during the more difficult action sequences. But the most exciting thing that's happened to Corey while shooting the series wasn't on the set at all.

"I had my friend Danny over," he says with an enthusiastic smile. "We were in Spain, we were sitting on a bed playing Connect Four, and all of a sudden we saw something moving on the bed. We were like, 'What's that!?' And we jumped off the bed and looked at it. It was a scorpion! It was big and brown. We were told it wasn't that dangerous, but we were still scared. Then they said, 'Do you want to go back in the tent?' We said, 'No, not anymore!' I think that was probably the scariest thing that's happened to us so far!"

✪ SEAN PATRICK FLANERY

Where Corey Carrier's episodes end, Sean Patrick Flanery's begin. As the dashing, heroic sixteen-year-old Indiana Jones, Sean continues to show us how the archaeologist/adventurer we all know came to be. Indy has seen more of the world than the average teenager. Leaving home to join the Belgian army during the fighting of World War I is only one of the many unusual

While danger awaits young Indy everywhere he goes, a promising career lies ahead for Corey Carrier, the actor who portrays him as a youngster.

Photo by Keith Hamshere copyright © 1991
Lucasfilm Ltd.

Actor Sean Patrick Flanery
ready for action.

Photo by Craig Blankenhorn copyright
© 1991 Capital Cities/ABC, Inc.

Photo by Keith Hamshere copyright
© 1991 Lucasfilm Ltd.

circumstances Indy finds himself in. He learns many valuable lessons about the horror of war, the incredible wonders that history holds, and the joy and pain of love.

"There's a lot more adolescence apparent in my character, and he's a lot more naive than Harrison Ford's character," Sean explains. "But as far as mannerisms and gestures, that's the stuff that I really tried to copy from Ford, like the way he puts his hat on or the way he wears it around girls, the way he cracks the whip—everything. I tried to emulate that as close as possible or incorporate that in my character. I just wrapped it all up and used what I could."

Since Indiana Jones was first portrayed by Ford, did Sean talk with the veteran actor and get some tips on how to play the character?

"No. Too bad, too, I'd love to meet him, but no. Rick McCallum, the producer, did give me copies of *Raiders of the Lost Ark*, *Temple of Doom*, and *The Last Crusade* and I watched each one of them, no joke, like twenty-five times to learn how he rode a horse, and how he walked, and how he turned around, etc.

"Nobody ever really said, 'We want you to emulate Harrison Ford,' but, you know, he's Indiana Jones. It's the only perception we've got of Indiana Jones, so I wanted to at least include some of that in my character."

Like so many people, Sean recalls standing in line at the theater back in 1981 to see the blockbuster hit *Raiders of the Lost Ark*. While countless moviegoers can relate to the excitement he felt during the opening scene when the giant boulder raced across the screen, most can't imagine what it must be like to play the part of Jones as a teen nearly eleven years later.

"My first encounter with Indiana Jones," recalls Sean, "was in the theater. I must have been ten years old, but it was the most exciting film I'd ever seen in my life.

The scene where the big ball chases him out of that tunnel stuck with me. . . . It's still with me. That was the talk of every classroom. 'Did you see *Raiders of the Lost Ark* yet?' I mean, the thought never even entered my mind that one day I'd be playing Indiana Jones. It's weird how stuff like that happens."

Born in Lake Charles, Louisiana, and raised in Houston, Texas, since the age of three, Sean Patrick Flanery wasn't always interested in acting. As any normal teenage boy does, he listened to rock music, was involved in sports, and was interested in cars. Acting was something that Sean got involved with in a roundabout way.

"I was going to the University of St. Thomas in Houston," the young actor remembers, "and there was a gorgeous girl who was taking a drama class. I dropped an English class, posthaste, and signed up for drama. I fell in love with drama . . . the girl ended up being a real flake." He laughs. "But I did all kinds of college theater and everything just stemmed from that."

After moving to Los Angeles, Sean paid his dues like most actors by waiting tables to pay the bills. He saved his money, had new head shots taken, and after eight months of looking, got an agent to represent him. He did a string of television commercials before winning roles in several movies. But Sean's shot at stardom was yet to come. In January of 1991 he was called in to audition for the role of Indiana Jones. After numerous callbacks and a meeting with George Lucas, Sean started getting excited. It wasn't until three months later that he was notified that he had won the role. "It had been slowly building up and I knew I was getting closer and closer and closer," Sean recalls, "and finally toward the last week, I pretty much knew I had it, but I didn't have the final word, so I couldn't sleep at night!"

After being cast, Sean was flown to London, England,

where he rehearsed for four months. "I got off the plane and it was pouring rain," he says. "For four months I didn't see a sunny day. There was nothing but clouds and rain. But everybody was incredibly nice.

"I spent two months in preproduction taking horse-back-riding lessons," he continues. "I got pretty good. I did all kinds of trick riding, you know, standing up in the saddle, jumping on the horse from a full gallop, running next to it, jumping on, jumping off, jumping back on, jumping over cliffs—I mean, all kinds of stuff. I learned a lot about stunts. How to do stunts, how to do falls, how to do punches. What the camera reads as opposed to what really looks like a punch. Gee, I took Spanish lessons. I've learned all kinds of languages from Arabic to Greek, Italian, Ancient Greek, German, French. I've even taken some piano lessons and some nautical lessons."

While he is quite an Indiana Jones movie fan, Sean says he is pleased that the television series has its own unique style.

"The movies were pretty much action from start to finish, and that's not to say they lack intellectual depth, but the TV series kind of integrates both. It's very multileveled viewing. There's a lot of action, there's romance, but there's kind of a moral to the story, as well as a good factual lesson to every episode. All the charac-ters that I come into contact with are where they were during that time period, associating with the people that they actually associated with."

In the television series we see just how much Indiana Jones loves history. It's because of this love that he decides to become an archaeologist. But how about Sean Patrick Flanery? Has he ever had much of an interest in history or archaeology?

"I studied a little bit here and there in high school,"

he responds. But apparently his studies were not like his firsthand experiences on the set. "We shot in Wales with some old land structures and castles and things that were from the eleven hundreds. It was so cold and damp, and leaning out the window, I was thinking, 'I wonder whose elbows were leaning on this brick windowsill back in the eleven hundreds? Was it some knight with a spear just yanked out of his chest? Was he bleeding?' You just never know. Those kinds of thoughts race through your brain. Living in the United States, you rarely see anything over two hundred years old. It's so brand new. You go to London, and there's buildings, like the hotel I'm staying in, which were built in seventeen something. It has kind of sparked a new interest. I can't say that I ever had an interest growing up, but it's probably from lack of information about it. I mean, I was just never around any of it."

From Prague, Czechoslovakia, to London, England, to Almería, Spain, to Lamu and Nairobi in Kenya, Sean Patrick Flanery has been given a once-in-a-lifetime opportunity to see the world through the making of *The Young Indiana Jones Chronicles*. But even so, the cast and crew work on the kind of grueling schedule associated with most production shoots. Sean's average day begins about six in the morning. After having a bowl of cereal or a quick snack, it's on to the makeup chair to have his fake scar—fashioned after the real scar Harrison Ford has on his chin—put on. Then it's back to his trailer to get into costume and wait to be called for shooting. During that time Sean reads his script to make sure he has his lines memorized. After a full morning of filming, the cast and crew break for lunch and then it's back to work. "It's strictly shooting and eating until we wrap," explains Sean. "But the whole time they're lighting the set and getting everything set up, there's all kinds of

19

things going on to keep us busy because there's a lot of time spent waiting—card games, jokes, cutting up, some basketball tournaments. You name it, it's there."

Sean also took time out to tell us a bit about the problems and dangers filming in foreign countries posed. While every step is taken to ensure that no one is in any danger, when you're filming a show like *The Young Indiana Jones Chronicles* in exotic locations and have some fast-paced action sequences, anything can happen. And Sean has had his share of thrills and spills!

"There've been some scary moments," he says with a chuckle. "I guess the first scary moment I had was when we were shooting the Movie-of-the-Week, the Mexico episode, and I was doing a tracking shot. I was on a horse, Hurricane—the black horse that was Harrison Ford's horse. He rode it in all the Indiana Jones movies. It's really a famous horse. I'm at full-speed gallop behind this tracking vehicle, and I'm reaching out with my right hand, holding the reins with my left hand, trying to grab these dresses that one of Pancho Villa's Villistas stole from a seamstress. So I'm chasing after them trying to get these dresses back and, well, I got Hurricane a little too close to the back of the tracking vehicle. His hoof clipped the back bumper and his front hoof just went under his belly. He nosed down into the sand. I flew over his head, the tracking vehicle kept going, but it was really scary. I landed on my feet. Never even slid down, never got a scrape, but my heart was thumping.

"The most challenging thing I had to do was swim down the Tana River in Africa and not die," he says with a grin. "There were no alligators, but there were crocodiles. We landed on this grassy runway—there's giraffes, rhinos, hippos, crocs, and baboons everywhere. We're floating down the river in canoes, and on the banks there's every kind of animal you can imagine. The next day we're shooting a scene, and the boat capsizes, and I'm swimming down the Tana River. The water's the color of chocolate milk. It's the most vile, disgusting, revolting fluid you've ever looked at, and I'm swimming in this stuff. The whole time everybody's been talking about parasites in the water that can kill you in thirty seconds . . . the next thing I know, I'm under it. I've got a six-pound revolver around my waist in a holster. I've got leather gaiters, leather boots on, a big helmet strapped on my head, and I'm swimming down this river, thinking, 'Oh, my God, what bank am I gonna swim to? Which one looks like it has less trees or shrubbery?' My heart's going a hundred and sixty miles a minute, and then, finally, a boat came and picked me up!"

As Sean described, the life of an actor can sometimes have its ups and downs! It's fair to say that it is far from average. And, sometimes, as Sean found out, it can be quite unusual.

"I've had olive oil poured all over me from head to toe," he remarks as he shakes his head, grinning. "It was for the fight scene with Claw. Actually, we used liquid dishwashing detergent. They poured it all over me . . . sudsy, completely sudsy. Dried my skin out like mad, because I was in this fifteen hours a day. It was in my hair. I smelled good, though. From that to . . . oh, gee, you name it, I've had to dance with the Czechoslovakian ballet company, and I was in a skimpy costume. I've had to beat guys up, go in fiery buildings, ride horses over cliffs, fall off horses, fall off boats, speak different languages, play the piano—all kinds of weird stuff."

Long days, hard work, and shooting all over the world are just some of the things Sean Patrick Flanery will remember most from this first season of filming *The Young Indiana Jones Chronicles*. But he not only has fond memories of a year filled with excitement, he also has high hopes for the adventure to continue.

✪ GEORGE HALL

We've introduced you to both Corey Carrier and Sean Patrick Flanery in this chapter, but we've yet to meet the Indiana Jones we see at the beginning and end of each episode. His name is George Hall, and he's the actor that plays Indy today at ninety-three. Having seen a lifetime of adventure and excitement, Old Indy is as charming and appealing as he was in his youth!

"I was so delighted when I found out I had won the role of the older Indiana Jones," says Hall. "It's a wonderful opportunity. I think the idea of playing a man who has been known as a hero to the audience, in his final years, reminiscing about the time of his youth before he became a hero, is fascinating.

"Indy at ninety-three is a feisty old guy and is never hesitant to tell someone what he thinks of their behavior if it is obviously mean-spirited," George continues. "He's heroic in the sense that he's past the age of caring whether people appreciate what he's saying or not. He's old enough to know that the truisms are the truisms and should be believed because they are true. He's a good storyteller and he makes people want to listen to him and learn from listening to him. And then they go on and learn something else and continue the process of learning.

"I'm playing a character who's been all over the world, learned all sorts of things, and lived a good life as a result of that kind of knowledge. He's not like his father, Henry Jones, Sr., who is a professor of medieval literature, and a book-learning man. Indy is more of a zoologist, paleontologist, geologist, and he's out there doing things. So his education is different from his father's. It's almost a swashbuckling kind of education and one that makes him fascinating and charming. The challenge of playing Jones at age 93 is to make him interesting so that when he tells a story, people don't go, 'Oh, my God, here he goes again!' "

Having had a lifetime of acting experience, George Hall fulfills that challenge with ease. A graduate of the Neighborhood Playhouse School of Theater in New York, he has performed in over nineteen Broadway shows. He has worked with such Hollywood names as Carol Channing and Richard Gere and has made appearances on several soap operas in New York. He also appeared in the motion picture *Johnny Be Good*.

Hired more for his acting ability than for a resemblance to Harrison Ford, George Hall states, "I don't think I look much like Harrison Ford. The point is, if Laurence Olivier had lived to ninety-three, he might have looked a great deal different from his younger, Shakespearean days. So one shouldn't expect to look like one did when one was thirty . . . I'm not really concerned about the fact that I don't look like what everybody thinks he should look like. . . . I look like a man of ninety-three. But the makeup is really quite remarkable, even at close range. . . . Actually, I think the makeup does give me a resemblance to Harrison, certainly from a profile. He has a stronger chin than I have, but, you know, people shrivel when they get old," he says, laughing.

Although fans will recognize Old Indy's trademark brown fedora, at ninety-three he's traded his leather bullwhip for a walking stick with a brass handle shaped like an eagle's head. But there are more changes to Indy's outward appearance as well.

"I wear a patch over my right eye," explains George, "and a scar down my forehead. We assume that my right eye has been damaged. The scar continues down my right cheek and off to the side. And I wear my glasses over the patch, so it looks kind of romantic and rather strange and silly all at the same time!"

Not only do George Hall and old Indiana Jones share the same appearance and voice, they also share a love for the past.

"I do share his fascination with history," says George, "but I don't have the knowledge that his character has. I also have a fascination with nature. I'm no expert, but I do love the great outdoors."

Wilmington, North Carolina, is the location George and the Young Indy crew have been shooting the beginning and end scenes. The veteran actor recalls his first day of filming with great clarity.

In this episode Old Indy comes to the rescue of an old lady getting into a tussle with a young punk. He is hauled off to jail for assaulting the punk, but not before he tells him a story about World War I. "I felt good, I learned my lines, and I knew what I was doing. I wasn't nervous because I'm not playing the Indiana Jones that people all know from going to the movies. I'm playing a man, ninety-three, who is an Indiana Jones of another time and era," George concludes with a warm smile. "I want to be the Indiana Jones people love now."

2

The Supporting Cast of Characters

⭐ **MARGARET TYZACK**

In the first two-hour movie of *The Young Indiana Jones Chronicles*, Professor Henry Jones informs his wife and his son, Indy, that he has accepted the offer of a series of guest lectures in universities around the world. Young Indy is, of course, excited at the prospect of traveling. What he doesn't realize, however, is that he will be accompanied by the very strict and stern tutor, Helen Seymour. At first Indy doesn't really like Helen, whose watchful eye and hard-work attitude make it difficult for him to sneak off and have some fun. Later he realizes she taught him important lessons in life and stimulated his love of history. Margaret Tyzack, the actress who brings Helen Seymour to life, agrees that her character does have a major influence on Young Indy.

"Some people say to me, 'Don't you think she's rather hard on Indy?' And I say no, she is a Victorian lady and the thought of a child is, initially, rather dismaying to her. She's used to teaching adults, not children. Most Victorians believed that children should be seen and not heard. They thought of children as young minds to be formed and educated and molded. Victorian children who were fortunate enough to receive any education at all were in a classroom that was run very strictly. Perhaps Helen is a little firmer than other people were because she never dealt with children before in her life. And she does initially say, 'I'm not a governess, I'm a tutor.' I think Indy and she eventually come to respect each other, and as he grows up he realizes what an influence she had on him."

Margaret goes on to say that there was a certain discipline in the classrooms of that era, as well as a readiness to seize every learning opportunity that was presented. "You did not talk and did not wander around the room. There was a sort of quiet atmosphere in which to work. But as far as imparting knowledge, schools covered everything. And if you traveled to another country during that time, you would look into its history and make use of that history. There were also so many amazing inventors that came out of the period in which our series takes place. The Victorians and Edwardians were quite astonishing people. They also believed that a child was capable of everything. They didn't put a limit on what they thought he or she could cope with."

The Young Indiana Jones Chronicles has taken Margaret all over the globe, where she has seen some of the worlds great wonders. One memory she won't soon forget was her first sight of the ancient pyramids in Egypt and the difficulty she had climbing them for the two-hour pilot!

"There was such an intense heat there at the pyramids, and they seemed to pulse with the midday sun," she recalls. "I was very surprised to see the height of each step of the pyramids. They're very, very high. There's no way you can think of them as steps! It wasn't easy to climb them! And everything I had to do was in my Edwardian costume, which is very uncomfortable. That's what women wore in that day."

Helen Seymour is one of the few characters who ties the two different time periods in *The Young Indiana Jones Chronicles* together. We first meet her in the eight-year-old Indy's adventures and then meet up with her again in the London episode with the teenage Indy. Because of this, Margaret Tyzack has had the opportunity to work with both of the actors playing Young Indiana Jones. So what is her impression of these two young men?

"My impression of Sean is that he is an intelligent, hardworking, humorous, and courteous young man," she responds. "And as far as Corey is concerned, one could describe him by the same words but add to it, because of his youth, a ravenous curiosity about absolutely everything in the world and everything he comes across. There's nothing he doesn't want to read, nothing he doesn't want to know—it's not always restful," she says with a laugh. "My son is twenty-seven and it brings back memories of how things used to be when he was young!"

Margaret has had a long career in the performing arts and, over the years, has earned the respect of her fellow actors. She has worked in television, film, and theater and with the prestigious Royal Shakespeare Company in England. In 1990, Margaret won the respected Tony Award for her performance in the Broadway play *Lettuce and Lovage*. Her past credits include the ground-breaking BBC series *The Forsyte Saga*, which was the television series that introduced the BBC's programs to the world, and *I, Claudius,* in which she played the Roman emperor Claudius's mother, Antonia. Yet with all the projects that Margaret has been involved in, none matches the complexity and scope of *The Young Indiana Jones Chronicles*.

"I won't forget all the wonderful places I went with this show," the veteran actress says. "I would say this is an actor's dream come true!"

⭐ RONNY COUTTEURE

As we grow up, friends play an important part in our lives. They are the ones with whom we share our problems and with whom we have some of the most memorable experiences of our lives. But good friends are hard to come by when you spend your teens traveling to some of the most remote places in the world. It's safe to say, then, that Young Indy never thought he would meet one of his lifelong best friends while riding side by side with Pancho Villa's band of Mexican bandits.

Rémy Baudouin is a likable character who finds himself in some dangerous situations alongside his companion Indiana Jones. It's because of Rémy that Indy leaves Mexico to fight in the Belgian army in World War I.

The actor that brings Rémy so wonderfully to life is the character actor Ronny Coutteure, who, like Rémy, is Belgian.

"Rémy is a good guy," the actor states. "He's quite tender, and yet, on the other hand, he's also a man of action. He knows what he wants. He helps Indy to become a great person. He educates him in a certain way. He teaches him some dangers and tells him how to handle women, which he really doesn't know about any more than Indy! So he's quite a funny character. He's never satisfied. He does things in a new way. He's a hero, but he doesn't want to be a hero."

Coutteure, who is forty years old, lives in Paris, France. He's been acting for over twenty years. He's performed in a number of TV films in France, Switzerland, and in his native Belgium, where he is very well known. He is also a comedian and has performed extensively in his own one-man shows. Although Ronny has had a great deal of show-business experience, nothing prepared him for his experience on *The Young Indiana Jones Chronicles*.

"You know, English is not my native language, French is," he says. "I'm Flemish, which is like Dutch, so I prepare a week before. Every week I learn my lines for the following week and then every day I say them over and over. It's very important to say your lines naturally. And for me, the only way is to say them over and over. After that, when I come on the set, I try to forget it because it's also important to be ready for what can happen. I try to be free of my lines and see if I can invent something which can help. You must do both. You must be very well prepared and then have some invention, too."

Since Ronny has been shooting all over the world, often very far from his home in France, his wife has journeyed with him on the production. This is something that makes them both feel more comfortable.

"Rémy is such an important part of the series that I'm shooting quite a bit. I'm a long way from home, and my wife and I don't have any children, so this has truly been an adventure. I think it's important when you are far away from home, that you are together . . . it's kind of a security for me."

When all is said and done, Ronny has had the experience of a lifetime working on *The Young Indiana Jones Chronicles*.

"I've learned things about history and I've learned things about filmmaking, too," he says with a smile. "It's a different way of filming than we have in France. It's very interesting for me to see how an American production works. It's also very interesting for me as an actor because we have different approaches to acting than American actors. It has sometimes been very surprising!"

✪ LLOYD OWEN

Lloyd Owen has the difficult task of playing a character that was first created by one of Hollywood's biggest names. As Professor Henry Jones, originally played by Sean Connery in *Indiana Jones and the Last Crusade*, Lloyd has a unique opportunity to bring something new to the character while working from a blueprint already established by Connery. Lloyd doesn't naturally speak like Sean Connery, but he learned to imitate his accent by listening to many of his movies. It's been a thrill for Lloyd, who has admired the veteran actor for a long time.

One other aspect of Professor Henry Jones's character that came out in *The Last Crusade* as well as in the new series is Henry's love for medieval history. In the TV series, as in the film, we find Professor Jones interested in researching the myth and reality of the Holy Grail—the cup used by Christ at the Last Supper. Much to his pleasure, Lloyd Owen shares Henry's interest in the history of the middle ages.

"I studied 'The Knight's Tale' by Geoffrey Chaucer, which talked about the medieval chivalry code, which is the subject of a book Professor Jones has published. So, yes, I do share his love for history."

Aside from taking pride in his research on the Holy Grail, Professor Jones also takes pride in his son. Despite his desire to study everything concerning the legendary cup, he still takes time out for Young Indy. He's given Indy the chance of a lifetime to journey all over the world. It's because of Professor Jones that Indy has the opportunity to meet some of the greatest people of the twentieth century. Indiana's love for archaeology was inspired, in part, by his father.

"I believe Henry was a good father," says Lloyd. "I think that's obvious by the way Indy has turned out. He even said in the film that he's not the kind of father that says, 'Eat your food, go to bed, brush your teeth!' He's not that kind of guy at all. He's a very liberal parent for the 1900s."

When asked how he would compare father with son, Lloyd responded, "I think the stubbornness and sense of purpose is in both Indy and Henry, and their understanding of cultures all over the world. Actually, what's great about this entire series is that it is very open to all cultures and that's specifically true in the episode we did in India."

After months of shooting in various countries, Lloyd has enough memories to fill up a book. One of the most humorous memories for him is an experience he had in Egypt.

"This is my famous Egypt story," he says, laughing. "There's a great market in Cairo, Egypt. It's a big bazaar, and Ruth De Sosa, who plays Anna Jones, Joseph Bennett, who plays Lawrence of Arabia, and I went shopping there. All of a sudden a man with about three teeth came up and said, 'I show you leather boots.' We gave in and went to see the leather boots, which were very

31

ugly—gaudy gold and electric-blue boots. So we turned those down. He was a very friendly man and he said, 'I'm not a guide, but do you know Yorkshire?' We said, 'Yes, we know Yorkshire,' so he continued, 'My father works in Yorkshire.' He was trying to get friendly with us. And he said, 'I'm not a guide, but this place is for tourists. I'll take you to a special place for Arabs where you have one row of spices, one row of perfume, one row of cotton.' We said fine, and off we went.

"We were taken to an absolutely spectacular spice market that was all underground, and had huge canvas sacks filled with all kinds of wonderful spices. You were almost sneezing, it was so strong. He took us to one store and asked me if I wanted some of the herb called saffron, which is very expensive. I thought I would bring some home to my wife, who is a great cook. He decided to give it to me in powder form and he said, 'I'll charge you the equivalent of twelve or thirteen pounds [which is approximately $6.72 in U.S. dollars] for about five ounces.' So we bought some other things, and as we left, a very large, pregnant Arab woman looked at us and let out a big laugh! On the way back we stopped at the market where we were earlier and there was a spice stack. I thought I would just inquire as to how much five ounces of saffron would be. And the man said to me, 'Fifty pence—which is approximately twenty-three cents in U.S. dollars!' So I tried to find the man with three teeth in his head to knock the rest out," he says with a laugh.

"But he had disappeared. As we were leaving the market I saw some loofahs on a stand. I said, 'Oh, look, some loofahs.' And this completely different man came from behind me and said, 'Loofahs? You want loofahs? Do you know Yorkshire? My father works in Yorkshire. I'll take you to special place—one row of spices, one row of cotton, one row of perfume.' And this time I said, 'No thanks!' Finally, when I got home, I found out the saffron was really a different spice altogether called tamarind! Besides that, though, I had a great time in Egypt. But I won't forget that incident!"

✪ RUTH DE SOSA

"My mom was quite a lady," says the ninety-three-year-old Indiana Jones. "She was the sweetest, smartest, most wonderful woman who ever lived. . . ."

Indeed, Mrs. Anna Jones deserves as much credit for Indy's sense of adventure and love of history as his father, Professor Jones. Anna is a compassionate and caring mother who does her best to see that Indy experiences all the wonders the world has to offer. As she travels to various countries with her husband and son, we see that she is a woman of intelligence and class who appreciates some of the finer things in life.

The actress that portrays this remarkable woman is the lovely and talented Ruth De Sosa. The role of Anna Jones is the kind that actresses wish for—a strong and intelligent woman who travels all over the world. In real life the role has taken Ruth De Sosa to Africa, China, England, and Czechoslovakia, where she has worked with talented professionals, both in front of and behind the camera. Not surprisingly, the actress has nothing but love and respect for the character she brings to life.

"I think that Anna is a very good mother and wife," she states. "I think she's very, very excited by the journey. She was raised in America, and the chance to see the world is a dream come true. Through her travels, she grows a lot and learns a great deal about different

33

Photo by Craig Blankenhorn copyright © 1991 Capital Cities/ABC, Inc.

Professor Jones (Lloyd Owen), Helen Seymour (Margaret
Tyzack), Anna Jones (Ruth De Sosa), and young Indy (Corey
Carrier) pose for a family portrait.

T. E. Lawrence, tutor Helen Seymour, and Pierre Duclos look on as Indy learns a lesson he uses later in life.

people. It's very exciting to her, she wouldn't want to stay home and settle down."

Although Anna appears in many episodes, there is very little written about the character. To some actresses this would pose a problem, but for Ruth it opens the door for her own interpretation, with the basic foundation of the character established by George Lucas. It's exciting and difficult all at the same time.

"I really have come up with ideas in my mind as to what Anna is like," the actress says. "I don't know why, but when I read a scene, I just suddenly know who she was. And I'm glad the casting people thought I knew who she was, too! But I do have my difficult moments. You know, she dies very soon—within three years— when Indiana is only twelve years old. I think that she is very full of life and you're very sad when she's gone because she had so much energy, so that's what I try to portray."

Ruth also believes Indy's natural desire to learn more about the past can be credited, in part, to his mother's love of knowledge and adventure. "I think she is definitely Indy's guiding light," Ruth relates. "I think that part of his adventurous spirit comes from Anna."

3

Behind the Scenes with Producer Rick McCallum

Organizing and preparing a project the size of *The Young Indiana Jones Chronicles* is an incredibly difficult task. It requires an individual with the ability to make important, and sometimes quick, decisions. It also requires meticulous planning and an ability to oversee all aspects of the production from start to finish. In Hollywood, the people who perform this important job are called producers. The producer's role is crucial to the success of any film or television series. So naturally, Lucas wanted a hardworking individual with vast experience to push the production along regardless of the setbacks it might face. The man he found to perform this important job is producer Rick McCallum.

McCallum has a long history of working in television and film. Based in London, England, he has also produced such projects as the award-winning BBC series *The Singing Detective, Track 29, Strapless, Dreamchild, Castaway*, and *Pennies from Heaven*. He has also produced over twelve films in Great Britain. McCallum was first approached to produce the *Chronicles* by *Last Crusade* producer Robert Watts. He gave Rick a simple outline of George's plans to shoot in various countries with a small crew for very little money—something Rick had been trying to do in England for the last seven years. He was immediately interested.

"I met George in March and started on the show immediately," says Rick. "I prepared for just over a year. First of all I had to find seven writers both in the United States and England. Most of the writers are English. That took about four months because I met maybe sixty or seventy writers. Trying to narrow that down to six or seven was a very long and tiring job. That went from about March to July. From July to September I started interviewing and probably met a hundred English directors—almost every director working in England. In September, we had a one-month-long story conference with all the writers in San Francisco. From those basic outlines, which were very structured, I began the search for all the locations we would be shooting in. That lasted about four months. In January of '91, I put a team together, and that's when we started official preproduction for four months. We finally began shooting May thirteenth."

Fortunately, Rick McCallum was well prepared for the enormity of the project because of his previous experience.

"I had worked on a BBC television series called *The Singing Detective*, which shot for twenty-six weeks and also a series called *Blackeyes,* which shot for the same amount of time," Rick reveals. "But nothing has ever been set up in the fashion of the *Young Indiana Jones Chronicles*. We're making this for the same price as an average action-adventure-series episode and we shoot ours in almost fifteen countries. We're shooting for almost forty-four weeks nonstop."

The actual process of bringing a Young Indiana Jones episode to life requires the efforts of hundreds of people. Long hours are spent in each department to make Indy's adventures happen. And it all begins with a story from the creative mind of George Lucas.

"We have a story conference with all the writers," Rick reveals. "Basically, we all live together in a house near San Francisco. We eat, sleep, and stay together for one month and work from seven-thirty in the morning until seven-thirty at night. Every day we plot out an episode and then spend the next morning rewriting that episode. To do fifteen episodes in thirty days is very, very difficult. Then we rewrite for about six months. One of the things we insisted upon for this series is that we have all the scripts done and finished before I started preparation so we didn't go through this madness of rewriting up to the last minute and incurring huge production costs because things weren't available. All the writers are working together on each script. They don't know which one they are going to do. Then, at the very end of the period, we assign the episodes. They have two months to come up with their first draft—they each do two episodes. At the end of the fourth month, we meet and we spend three weeks in a room together again and each person has to defend their script against the others—everybody gets to read everybody's scripts. There are rewrites again after that. We do the exact same process again and then we lock into the scripts.

"The minute we've locked into the scripts," he continues, "I start to prepare. I close in on the director we're going to use and then start to scout locations. I've already, during that period, set up the foundations of working in whatever country we'll be shooting in. All

Producer Rick McCallum keeping an eye on all aspects of the production.

the department heads go out to the locations, and because we're working nonstop, we have to do that on the weekends: we leave on Friday night and get back on Sunday night and go straight back to work on Monday."

Each episode of the *Chronicles* is shot within a three-week time span with the two actors playing Indy alternating, giving them each more time to rehearse. "After we've finished shooting, the footage is sent back to George in the States and they send us tapes of the assembly, the rough cut, and then the fine cut," says McCallum. "We go over it and make our notes and send it back to San Francisco, they make the adjustments or we argue about it intensely. Then we finally log off. And right now we are in the process of scoring the music. Our composers are Laurence Rosenthal and Joel McNeely. They take turns on each episode."

McCallum works closely with George Lucas all through the production, even on location, talking with him four or five times a week. Together they make the important decisions that have to be made to keep the series running along on schedule. Rick is the man-in-the-field who reports to George on the crew's progress.

"The thing about George that I love is that we work very, very closely together and there's a kind of shorthand we use; we don't need to discuss a lot," says Rick. "We both base our decisions on our first instinct, which, luckily, has been pretty good. I talk to him every week from wherever I am. We're pretty much in sync about all the major decisions. He has a very strong point of view and I have a very strong point of view, and usually it's never caused us any problems whatsoever.

"George is very, very strong on the story development, initial idea, and the overall creative aspects of the series," Rick continues. "That's one job you can do in San Francisco. What he also does is stay on top of the postproduction. My job is really preproduction and the physical production of the film. Neither one of us can be in two places at the same time and we both have different jobs. It's not that we both can't do each one, it's just that he also has another empire to run. And since we're doing all the postproduction in San Francisco, he can monitor and be my eyes, because where we are, we don't get rushes for two or three weeks after we finish shooting things. But he gets them right away and then he can make comments to me and I can make the adjustments. We are so in sync about what it is we are trying to make; it hasn't been a problem at all. It's relieving on one hand and kind of energizing on another. It's kind of freed us all."

One interesting aspect of Rick's job is scouting for the locations where they will shoot the series. This has literally taken him around the world in order to find the perfect areas to film. But it's not an easy task. There is more to consider than just the look of the location. Rick must take into consideration how far from civilization the locations are and whether he can get to the location with relative ease, including the transportation of food and water. One location that required a great deal of scouting was China.

"I went to China a year before we filmed there," says the *Chronicles* producer. "I just had a general look around. The places I would've needed to get to in China for the story are literally thousands of miles away from any kind of civilization whatsoever. So I had to find unique locations that are specifically indigenous to the China of the period of 1908, and also find a very large metropolitan center where I could house the crew. I didn't have much luck a year ago, but then I sent back an art director about six months later and found what I was looking for. It took us about eight months to get permission. I came out about a week before we started shooting just to finalize the rest of the Chinese crew.

"Getting permission to shoot in some of these countries can take a long time," he continues. "India took nine months and Africa took about three months. In most countries, like the United States or England, you don't need the government's permission to shoot. But there is still a whole other world that exists where basically three quarters of the world's population lives in a completely and utterly different state than we do."

Although both the films and the TV series take place in exotic locations, the two productions do have their differences. How would producer Rick McCallum describe these differences?

"The films are like a fictionalization of a real person, but in the series we're doing the 'real' person. The films are completely action-oriented. They have a very, very small and minor plot—something happens and Indy has to do incredible things to save the world. What can we do for the next hour and a half to move this thing at the most lightning speed? Whereas the *Chronicles* is totally about character development. There is some action, but mostly it's about a young boy who learns about life, which is unusual for global television. Everything he learns about, from his relationship to food, women, ethics, morality, to the way he interrelates with people, he learns from the rest of the world, not America.

"One of our goals," Rick maintains, "was to make this series look like a feature film. Another goal was certainly to develop the character, which is something you can do on European television, but is very, very difficult to do on American television.

"The basic idea for this series, which George has been working on for a long time," says Rick, "is to explore the character of Indiana Jones through this incredible period of history. Ultimately, the dream is to have fifty or sixty hours, so that you can walk into a video store and literally watch the story of a small boy, from the time he was eight, in 1908, right up to the end of the Second World War, dovetailing into the films. We show Indy meeting some of the most extraordinary people of this century and watching the most extraordinary changes— never actually influencing the history, but just being at that point where he acts as a catalyst for our understanding of the basic problems we have today, in terms of the environment, education, etc."

So does Rick McCallum believe the series will spark young people's interest in history?

"I hope so, but that's a huge task," he responds. "I would like the series to introduce people to the concept of another world outside of America. There is this vast group of people who live in such a completely different way and, often, live much more successfully than we do, certainly in terms of personal happiness. The whole concept of language is also something that both George and I really hope starts to spark some interest. Each episode has people speaking in a different language— French, Spanish, Chinese, etc. Indy speaks with them in their language and we see the translation of that. You know, we are such a small minority in the whole world. There are huge influences taking place. In 1992, all the barriers in Europe will be broken down and it will be one community with close to 450 million people. That's 200 million more people than the United States."

A project like *The Young Indiana Jones Chronicles* comes along very rarely in a producer's career. For Rick McCallum, the job of overseeing this massive production has been a joy mixed with its share of problems and difficulties. It has taken him all over the world, put him together with some of the most talented people working

The TV series provides a glimpse of the public and private moments of some very celebrated figures, including Albert Schweitzer (played by actor Friedrich Von Thun) . . .

Photo by Keith Hamshere
copyright © 1991
Lucasfilm Ltd.

Photo by Keith Hamshere copyright © 1991 Lucasfilm Ltd.

·. . . but it also features many unsung heroines, including the countless women who supported the suffragette movement.

Photo by Craig Blankenhorn copyright © 1991 Capital Cities/ABC, Inc.

in the entertainment industry worldwide, and given him a scrapbook of wonderful memories. Yet out of all these things, one element stands above them all.

"The best thing has been working with George Lucas," he says emphatically. "I've had the luxury of working with some of the most famous American directors and I have been disappointed by many of them—not so with George. I now know him as well as anybody. We've gone through some amazing things together and I've never seen him lose his cool. He is the only person in the business that puts all of his money back into his projects in every single way. Most of the time you never see the executive producer. But George spends as much time as I do on this series every day. He's relentless and obsessive in the best possible way. He's totally unmaterialistic: anyone else with that power and money would abuse it. It's never about ego, it's always about the series. He has the most amazing story sense of anyone I've ever worked with. Knowing him has been the most extraordinary experience!"

4

Bringing Young Indy's Adventures to Life

Each week, as we watch a new adventure in *The Young Indiana Jones Chronicles* unfold on our television sets, it seems as if we are watching real life. But what we don't see is all the hard work that goes into making up Indy's adventures. As you can imagine, they don't just happen. They are well-thought-out stories planned more than a year in advance.

Each episode starts with a story that comes directly from the mind of George Lucas. Then writers are brought on board to flesh the story out and write the words the actors will say.

"Doing the stories, I work with the research department here," explains Lucas. "I'll work for six or eight months setting the foundation, then all the writers come together. For three weeks we pitch the stories, laying them out in detail with the writers. Then they write the screenplays. That's the fun part. The stories just pop into your brain. It's a bubbling-caldron thing. It's the kind of thing that gives me the excitement to go ahead.

I'm only doing this because I can't stop it from happening. It sort of bubbles out of my brain, and there's nothing I can do about it. The truth is, I haven't had this much fun doing anything since *Raiders of the Lost Ark*.

"I have confidence that the writers are all very professional and really know why we're doing this and what's behind it," Indy's creator continues. "They come back, and the scripts are close to what I had in mind, and then I get to rewrite the scripts and work with the writers to help it get closer to what I want."

Some of the finest writers from around the world have been assembled to work on this series. The list includes such accomplished playwrights, screenwriters, and mystery novelists as Rosemary Anne Sisson, Reg Gadney, Jonathan Hales, Matthew Jacobs, Gavin Scott, Frank Darabont, and Jonathan Hensleigh.

Writer Matthew Jacobs has high praise for the way George Lucas works with his writers as a team.

"It's been inspiring," he says. "Personally, I've never done this before, working in a group. But when you're working this way, you don't know who in the group is going to write which screenplay. So we all go through the process, caring about every story, because we might have to write that one. We write out a little list of our favorites. We don't know . . . maybe we're not going to get the ones that are our favorites, but we did last year. This is the way I'd like to work on other projects. I think it's a shame that writers can't talk more to each other and be able to exchange ideas."

As the process began, many of the writers were overjoyed to be working on a project they believed in. A project that has a message yet is thoroughly entertaining—the kind of project George Lucas is known for.

"The series is really what George is trying to accomplish and we're in a position of supporting his vision," remarks writer Frank Darabont. "It's an exciting vision, which is terrific. He sees it as being a chance to sort of illuminate things a little bit. I love the fact that we are getting glimpses into things that generally aren't fed to us on television—historical events, historical figures, their philosophies. The whole series seems to be about a young man's influences—what shaped this guy's mind as he was growing up, the people that he met, the events that occurred. In a way my theory is that Young Indy is definitely Young George Lucas, and he is getting to act out physically now by sending Indy all over the world. I think Young Indy is visiting all the people and places that George visited in books when he was a kid."

As many of the writers on the series have explained, each was given the opportunity to write the episode that appealed to them most after collectively brainstorming ideas. Naturally, different episodes appealed to different writers for different reasons: some liked romance more, others liked action, and still others liked such serious topics as the horrors of war, or the differences in world religions, and so on. In the following paragraphs several of the writers discuss their individual episodes and why they chose to write them.

Jonathan Hensleigh wrote the India episode. In this episode Indy, his parents, and his tutor, Helen Seymour, travel to Benares, India, in the summer of 1908. On their first day there, Indy is supposed to be studying geometry, but instead he takes a walk to see the sights and meets a group of Indian boys playing cricket, one of whom is the thirteen-year-old Jiddu Krishnamurti, who later becomes a world-famous metaphysical thinker and religious teacher.

"This episode is an explanation of the world's religions," says writer Hensleigh. "Benares is the most holy city in India, and all the religions are kind of featured there prominently—you know, there's an enormous Islamic mosque, there's a Buddhist temple, there's an Episcopalian church, there's all kinds of Hindu temples. The India episode will actually be the most controversial of any, I think, because any studio executive will tell you that you can't show anything that has to do with religion on American television. And this one hour is a comparative study of the world's religions, basically, with Indiana Jones."

Writer Matthew Jacobs was attracted to several different episodes. He ultimately chose the Kenya 1909 episode and the Vienna 1908 episode—two very different stories but both with an important point to make.

"I particularly wanted the Kenya episode," recalls Jacobs, "because the idea of doing an ecological adventure story was very strong. Teddy Roosevelt is a great character, and the relationship between Indy and the Maasai boy was something that I knew I could write well, and I knew would be great. Also, it's interesting—this story is about language as well. Whenever Indy travels, he tries to learn the language, and so you're talking about communication between two boys from totally different cultures—how Indy learns from this boy and his world and how he manages to solve Roosevelt's problem—Roosevelt is looking for a species, he can't find it, but then Indy finds it for him. In the bargain he gets chased by lions, gets stampeded by wildebeests—he has a great adventure. And so it seemed like an honest-to-goodness story—one I would want to watch."

English writer Rosemary Sisson's choice of episodes came down to two very different stories as well. One, set in China, required extensive research, but the other, set in England, was more familiar to her as the time period she wrote about in the British series *Upstairs, Downstairs.*

"I think the England episode is very simply a state-
ment that a woman can have a career," says Sisson. "It's
set in its own time, because it's not such a new message
for today, but it is looking back at a time when a woman's
principal objective was to marry and have children. If
she couldn't marry and have children—as many women
after the great war couldn't because their fiancés were
killed—then in a way she was a failure."

The other subject Sisson explores in this episode is
one that can be set in virtually any time period. It is the
age-old concept of timing in love. Sisson goes on to say,
"I think the charm of the England episode is that, in a
way, Indy is the right man at the wrong time, which is
something else that happens. His love, Vicky, admits
she'll probably never love anyone as much. They were
simply at the wrong time and place."

When it came to writing her second episode, set in
China, Rosemary utilized the Lucasfilm research department to help provide details about Chinese culture.
Since the episode deals with respect for other people's
cultures, having the characters act very much as they
would in that time and place was extremely important
to Rosemary.

"The moment I saw that the people were taken around
in sort of wheelbarrows," she says, recalling the research
into Chinese tradition, "I kept saying, this character in
our script, this acupuncture doctor, this very distin-
guished Chinese doctor has got to arrive in a wheelbar-
row, which is actually what would have happened. And
Indy's mother looks out, aghast, and thinks, 'This is the
man who's going to treat my child?' Really, until about
ten years ago, acupuncture was looked upon as mumbo
jumbo." Sisson's perceptions about human behavior
combined with diligent research are what made many
moments throughout her episodes so compelling.

Frank Darabont was another writer who felt that the Lucasfilm research department enhanced the telling of his story. He fondly refers to Debbie Fine of Lucasfilm as "the Terminator of research—a truly relentless soul." Frank could not be present at the first writers' meeting at Skywalker Ranch because he was busy in Los Angeles doing rewrites on the Disney film, *The Rocketeer*. But even though he got the left-over episodes, Frank says he really lucked out.

Apparently, Frank's first episode, which was initially supposed to be a one-episode show, got expanded into a two-parter because the source material provided by the research department was so vast and rich. The episode begins in December of 1916, in German East Africa. The Belgian and the British forces were pushing the Germans east to try to get them out of Africa. Indiana Jones and a group of fellow soldiers are given the assignment to trek across Africa and pick up a shipment of weapons and bring them back, which in 1916, is not an easy task because helicopters had not yet been invented then. In fact, in 1916, the only way to get across Africa was by train, boat, or walking. But the real problem in 1916 Africa was not so much battle casualties but . . . disease.

"This part of Africa was a terribly disease-ridden region, and still is," Darabont states. "So the story is really about Indy and these other soldiers on this sort of heart-of-darkness trek across Africa, as death by attrition due to disease is claiming many of the lives of these men . . . and leaving them behind . . . and finally getting to where the guns are and then trying to get back across the continent. And what happens from there is really fascinating. Indy meets the famous philosopher, clergyman, and physician Albert Schweitzer in the jungle, and he changes Indy's life in a very fundamental way. He is, in fact, a real person. He is an historical figure with some extraordinary things to say that change Indy's life a bit. It was a great episode to write."

The success of *The Young Indiana Jones Chronicles* clearly rests on the shoulders of many dedicated, professionals. But as you can see, it was the seven talented writers (some of whom were not featured here, but are every bit as important as those who were) who carried much of the initial responsibility. For it is the writers who first bring the characters to life on the written page.

"I guess, in a way, what's fun about this series is that you can show the character developing," explains Frank Darabont. "I think we're doing a pretty good job of not limiting ourselves to the thought 'Oh, well, he's Indiana Jones—he would never act this way, never run away from something, or never be emotionally affected by something. After all he is quite a bit younger than when we all met him in the three films. So it's fun to show you different sides of when he's younger and less assured, those moments when he can't figure something out or when he does figure something out and learns from it.

"Basically, he's a character who's trying to seek some base values by which to live. He's looking for a moral code. I guess he's looking for what everybody's looking for, which is sort of the unwritten set of rules that you carry around inside you—the conduct on how to live and how to treat others. What is just and what is not."

For many writers the greatest reward comes when an actor or actress interprets the written word into action and emotion. On the *The Young Indiana Jones Chronicles* there are many guest stars playing many famous people from the past. All of these actors draw upon their training, innate talent, and in many cases upon their own personal experiences to bring the writers' words alive. But for one actor, Mike Moroff, who plays Pancho

A single image conveys a thousand words.

Villa in the two-hour pilot, the words of writer Jonathan Hales were even more important than most. Moroff's grandfather actually rode with Villa's gang and Moroff also inherited several love letters written by Villa to his aunt. "My father grew up in Chilhuahua, Mexico, where Pancho Villa was from," says Moroff. "He was my father's hero." As Jonathan Hales will no doubt tell you, a writer could not ask for an actor to be more prepared to enliven his or her words than that!

After the scripts have been written and revised, it falls to actors such as Moroff and to the directors to bring the words on the page to life. Each episode utilizes a different director to do this.

"We have a wide range of directors," states George Lucas. "We have French, American, Danish, Australian, and British directors—directors from all over the world."

Enjoying the exchange with these talented directors, George Lucas travels to meet personally with each of them on location.

"I end up on location about every two or three weeks," Indy's creator says. "I've been to almost all the locations at one time or another. I usually try to get on location in between episodes, so when one director's finishing and another is starting, I can sort of deal with two directors at once. I can find out what's happened and what's going to happen. We sit here on top of the story. I'm the monitor of how far we can push the system and still have it work. Rick McCallum double-checks me on that because he's really the guy who's in the field and making it happen. It's been very difficult. We've had the normal logistical problems of being in very remote places, where there's a lot of sickness and a lot of danger in terms of just trekking around. We've also had one of our boats run aground in the river. It sank, and that put us back a day. But amazingly enough, we're still on schedule. So far we've overcome almost everything that's been thrown at us, which is a real tribute to the guys who are slogging away every day trying to bring this thing to reality."

One of the "guys" Lucas refers to is English director, actor, and comedian Terry Jones, who directed the Spain 1917 episode. Terry is well known to audiences all over the world as one of the original members of the British comedy series *Monty Python's Flying Circus*. He has also directed the hilariously funny films *Monty Python and the Holy Grail*, *Personal Services*, and *Erik the Viking*. Strangely enough, Terry got involved with *The Young Indiana Jones Chronicles* because of a phone that wouldn't stop ringing, he explains in his usual witty manner.

"Rick McCallum phoned me up and asked me if I'd be interested in doing it," he says with a smile, "and I said no. Then he rang me up again, and I said no, but he's a very persistent chap, and it started to sound like an intriguing idea! I sort of caught up with it, and I particularly liked the idea when I met George. I found the whole concept of using, I suppose, the most popular fictional character of the twentieth century very interesting."

As with every episode, Terry's show was filmed outside of the United States. Using the local talent and historic landmarks whenever possible gives the series an international feel. In the episode Terry directed, filming took place in Prague, Czechoslovakia, at Shepperton Studios in England, and in Barcelona, Spain.

Not only was Terry working behind the camera, he also appeared in the Spain episode as one of the bumbling spies. With such a rushed schedule, shooting in three different countries, and so much to do both in front of and behind the camera, what did Terry find most difficult?

"My head!" he exclaims. "I didn't realize I was going to have to cut my hair. I thought I could wear a short wig! Actually, the most challenging aspect was the pace. We were occasionally doing thirty, forty setups a day, and especially in Prague where we were shooting in a theater. We had an audience of five hundred actors to get through about thirty-five setups. It was quite grueling."

With the episode completed and the series well on its way, Terry Jones has the satisfaction of knowing he helped to get the show off the ground and that he gave the viewers what may be the most hilarious episode of the series.

In addition to Terry Jones the series has attracted some other very fine directors from around the world.

"Most of the directors we have on this series, I have known or worked with before," says producer Rick McCallum. "What's great is that I can get major film directors and serious art directors to come in and do this because they are not tied up for a long period of time. They can actually be working while they're developing something else. They can visit a really unique and wonderful country that they usually haven't been to and they can work with crews that they would never have had the opportunity to work with. So I have been very, very lucky. We have some of the greatest directors on this series. We have Jim O'Brien, who directed the award-winning *Jewel in the Crown*. We have Carl Schultz, who did the Australian film *Careful, He Might Hear You*, as well as Terry Jones, Gavin Millar, who did *Dreamchild* with me, and Simon Wincer, who directed *Lonesome Dove*. We also have the great director Nicolas Roeg, who's directing the Mata Hari episode, and a director by the name of Bille August—he is the Swedish director who did the film *Pelle the Conqueror*. I have this wonderful Indian director, Deepa Mehta, who did the critically acclaimed film *Sam and Me* and is directing our India episode, too. Rene Manzor whose credits include *The Passage* and *Pere Noel* is also directing for us, as is Vic Armstrong who was the second unit director of *Indiana Jones and the Last Crusade* and *Terminator 2* among other films. All our directors have been fantastic!"

One of the directors Rick McCallum mentioned is the very talented Carl Schultz. With many films to his credit, Carl can pick and choose his projects. But he was attracted to *The Young Indiana Jones Chronicles* because he is a great admirer of George Lucas and he has always loved the Indiana Jones movies. Carl's first two episodes dealt with the eighteen-year-old Indy—first in Mexico with Pancho Villa's gang of bandits and then in the much less action-oriented London episode in which Indy falls in love.

"The London-based episode is much more character-oriented," says Schultz. "It's the first time he falls in love. It's unlike any of the other Indiana Jones stories, but because of that, I think it's particularly interesting. He's a young man in love with all its joys and disappointments, hopes and fears."

Most of the filming for the Mexico episode was done in Almería, Spain—the same location used in *Indiana Jones and the Last Crusade*. Almería is an old movie town today, as many of the so-called spaghetti westerns were shot there, including *The Good, the Bad and the Ugly*. The town is like a museum, so many filmmakers are attracted to the site. "It's a good location," says Schultz, "but it's a very, very difficult place to work because of the heat and the dust. But I'm used to that, having worked in Australia for a long time.

"The interesting thing about this series," Schultz continues, "is that each story takes you to a different country and a different set of experiences. Just reading through the scripts, I thought they were brilliant. I learned something in each one. And I was entertained in each one, too. I hope that's what the series will do."

After the writers and directors have done their work, there is still more to be done. Once shooting is completed, the task of putting all the footage together rests with the editor. The two editors who work on the *Chronicles* are Edgar Burcksen and Louise Rubacky. In addition to editing the show, they are also responsible for coordinating the special effects.

"The effects for *The Young Indiana Jones Chronicles*

Executive Producer George Lucas with "cast" and crew.   *Keith Hamshere*

Filming all around the world, the series' actors learn to travel in style.

Keith Hamshere

Keith Hamshere

Pera Silva

Craig Blankenhorn

Keith Hamshere

Working with the likenesses of such historical
figures as Pancho Villa, General Patton,
General Pershing, Winston Churchill,
Pablo Picasso, and Lawrence of Arabia
is something to write home about.

Keith Hamshere

Keith Hamshere

Keith Hamshere

Keith Hamshere   *Keith Hamshere*   *Craig Blankenhorn*

David Farrell

After learning about valor, love, life, and people of all cultures will actor Sean Patrick Flanery turn his attention to directing?

Keith Hamshere

David Farrell

Keith Hamshere

Craig Blankenhorn

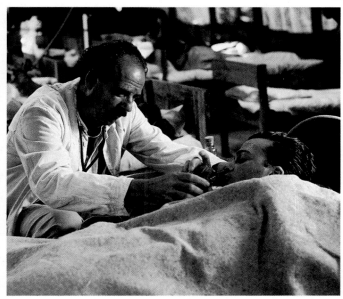

Keith Hamshere

Keith Hamshere

Maintaining his reputation as a master of special effects, Lucas plans a few surprises for Indy and viewers.

Keith Hamshere

Keith Hamshere

are totally different from anything you would expect normally," says Edgar. "For example, in a show like *Star Trek*, when you see a starship pass by the screen, you know that's a special effect because nothing like that exists today. But the effects for the *Chronicles* are the kind that you would never know are effects. We use matte paintings to make cities look like they did in the early 1900s. For example, we're doing a shot of London for one of the episodes and, of course, the city does not look today like it used to look back then. So we took a shot of modern-day London and blocked off the traffic on one particular street. We filmed people walking in period clothes and driving period cars on that street. Then a matte painter painted a picture of London 1908 at the same angle as our modern-day shot. Finally we cropped in the section of the street we shot with our actors and period cars so that it looks like the whole thing was shot in London in 1908. Basically, we mixed our live-action footage with the matte painting."

Another example of the realistic effects work done on the show can be seen in the Mexico 1916 episode. In a very dramatic scene Young Indy is thrown off his horse and surrounded by forty horsemen from Pancho Villa's gang. In reality what was shot was twelve horsemen surrounding actor Sean Patrick Flanery. Because of the high cost of renting horses and hiring extras, what Lucasfilm did was duplicate the Mexican bandits so that it looked like there were forty men surrounding Indy instead of the twelve actors that were actually there. "This is an effect that you would never notice was an effect," says Edgar.

Some of these effects are achieved by using a machine called the "Harry." The Harry is a compositing device that has been used extensively in commercials and in such films as *Terminator 2*. The Harry has not been used very much in episodic television, so *The Young Indiana Jones Chronicles* is really breaking new ground. Basically, the Harry is used to mesh two shots together—making them into one shot. It is a state-of-the-art machine that can create some very interesting effects.

In addition to the Harry, the effects editors also use a Macintosh computer that has a very sophisticated paint system allowing matte artists to paint directly in the computer instead of painting on glass. After the painting is completed, the artist can take it out of the Mac computer digitally, place it on an optical disk, and insert it in the Harry, where it is integrated into the actual footage that's been shot, just like the 1908 London city scene mentioned previously. The editors then put film grain on the painting to make it look like a moving picture and the whole thing looks like one shot. In this way art is integrated with actual film footage to create an entirely new scene. It's just another example of how Lucasfilm creates magic, whether it's on the big screen or the small screen, whether it's using spaceships or cities. It is truly amazing!

With such realistic effects, crew members were tempted to say, "Don't shoot until I'm out of here!"

5

Designing the Look of *The Young Indiana Jones Chronicles*

⭐ **CHARLOTTE HOLDICH**
Costume Designer

Costume designer Charlotte Holdich works very hard to design attractive, functional, and historically accurate costumes for the stars of *The Young Indiana Jones Chronicles*. She has the doubly difficult task of making new costumes that look as if they had been worn for years and searching for authentic period clothes that stand the test of being worn while filming this series!

"In England we're lucky," exclaims Charlotte, "because we have a lot of costumers that specialize in this. And so I use the real thing whenever possible because you do get an authentic feel. . . . But one of the problems, particularly with Sean's episodes, is that there are a lot of stunts and things, so you have to have five or six outfits that are the same. I choose a style, try them on Sean, photograph him, and send the photos to George. He makes his comments and lets me get on with it because we think along the same lines. I then get a fabric that has a period feel to it. I get enough of it to make five or six outfits. Often it has to be dyed and made up by a tailor. Shirts and ties must be made, too. Then it's sent off to be broken down so the whole thing doesn't look brand new. It's crumpled up and made to look authentic. That's a very specialized job."

Charlotte has worked on many shows for the BBC and has done her share of designing costumes for period pieces, but she admits that without question *The Young Indiana Jones Chronicles* is the most difficult and time-consuming project she's ever been involved with. It's like doing a feature film every week.

"I think that what's annoying about this job is that each episode is so visually interesting that I wish I had three months for each one instead of ten days. We have about a two-and-a-half-week turnaround time. And that's not a long time."

When it comes to the costuming of Indiana Jones, Charlotte must make various choices for the outfits of the character at different ages. For Corey Carrier's Indy, she dressed him in what ten-year-old boys living in 1908 would basically wear.

"The idea with Corey's Indy," she says, "is that we meet him first in Princeton and you see his life-style there. He looks like a nice young eight-year-old boy. I've got him in a sort of soft-colored brown suit and such things as spotted bow ties—a sort of informal look. Then he goes to England and meets his very strict governess and immediately she comments on his clothes and the way he stands. As soon as he's under her tutelage, he's changed his look and he's in stiff Eaton collars, and a

Norfolk suit—a heavy gray fabric that looks scratchy and uncomfortable, and indeed it is. He's also wearing these thick black stockings and laced-up boots. That's his image then. When he travels abroad to Egypt and wherever, he's wearing a similar suit made in a lightweight fabric, but again with this high collar, which is typical of young boys of that period. The governess tries to keep him looking as smart as possible. But being a young boy, he tends to get himself a bit grubby. George is very keen that whatever happens, he still looks like a young boy and tends to get grubby fingers and his clothes a bit messed up in his adventures."

For the older Indy Charlotte was given the opportunity to design many different costumes—from a Mexican bandito to an officer in the Belgian army. But despite all the costume changes there is one piece of his attire that is rarely missing—the trademark brown fedora that was introduced in the feature films.

"Well, it is Indy's trademark and he wears it quite often," remarks Charlotte. "Subsequently, in all our episodes, if he's not in some uniform, he's wearing his hat. I sort of have to incorporate this hat with all the various disguises and jobs that our Young Indy does. We're just about to film the Russian episode, where he joins the French Intelligence Corps and he's sent to the French embassy doing underground work in Russia 1917. I have to get the hat in there so it doesn't look too odd with a smart suit! It's a bit challenging."

One of the most interesting aspects of Charlotte's job is that she gets to design the costumes for some of the most famous people in history. She takes great pains to make sure the actors that are playing these historical figures are dressed accurately. She does this by researching hundreds of photos of these individuals to pick just the right look. She then must go searching for just the right clothing items to complete the look accurately.

Ironically, the greatest compliment a costume designer can receive is when the audience does not pay attention to the costumes in the show. They should not command attention but instead accentuate the story being told, adding to its credibility. In a period series like *The Young Indiana Jones Chronicles*, the costumes are an important part of making us believe we are stepping back in time to the early 1900s. But even if the costumes are so wonderful viewers are transported in time without even taking notice, we should not lose sight of the fact that professionals like Charlotte Holdich have worked very hard to ensure that *The Young Indiana Jones Chronicles* paints an accurate picture of the era Young Indiana Jones lives in.

✪ **GAVIN BOCQUET**
Production Designer

How do you make the surroundings of 1992 look like the surroundings of 1908 or 1917? The answer is to hire production designer Gavin Bocquet. Gavin's job is to design the extraordinary sets we see each week as well as to make sure the on-location landscapes show no signs of the modern age. Basically, anything that's seen behind the actors falls under Gavin's area of expertise. From the initial concepts, to sketches and drawings and, ultimately, to the final construction of the sets, Gavin is involved with it all. Sometimes it's not easy recreating the early 1900s.

"I don't think we could have achieved the look of this show without the help of Debbie Fine in the Lucasfilm research department," Gavin states. "When I came on

Whether setting a
table or setting a
mood, "Attention
to detail" was the
set, costume, and
production
designers' motto.

the series, we were almost twenty or twenty-five weeks away from shooting. If Debbie had not been doing the work she had been doing over the previous six months, we would not have been ready."

From Kenya to Spain to Egypt and Czechoslovakia, each episode features sets and outdoor locations that reflect the early 1900s. Some of Gavin's production designs are original. However, there are various times when Young Indy meets up with a famous, historical figure in their home or office. The sets must be historically accurate during these scenes.

"I think one of the most pleasing sets we've done is Albert Schweitzer's compound used in the Africa 1917 episode," says Gavin. "Certainly we don't have a huge amount of money for construction work, and yet, when we go to a country like Kenya, where our money is worth more to us, we can invest more on that side. It was obvious from the start that Schweitzer's compound was going to have to be something we would build from scratch. There was no way we would find that as a location. You automatically adjust your finances and budget to allow you to do that. One reason why that set was so enjoyable to make was because it was something real we had to re-create.

"If we're building a set," he continues, "I'll sit down and talk to the director and get an idea of where he wants to put the doors, etc. Actually, it's a great luxury to be able to build a set because you can have your door where you want it or you can have a hallway just where you need it. But, unfortunately, we haven't had a lot of money to build a lot of sets so we have been using locations. I'll scout for locations that I think will work— the geography is right in the room, the windows are in the right place and we have the right view out of the window and so forth. Then I'll go with Maggie Gray, the set decorator, and the director, and we'll discuss it. If it's right, there's little bits and pieces that we have to put together construction-wise. It's then handed over to Maggie to decorate."

On a feature film the production designer must spend long hours and work incredibly hard to design the appropriate sets that reflect what is in the script. But on *The Young Indiana Jones Chronicles,* the hard work and effort put into the production design is practically doubled because time is one luxury that Gavin Bocquet does not have. "It's an interesting exercise for a lot of people on the project," he says, "because you have to almost trust your instincts. Your first or second ideas are the ones that will count because you don't really have the time to think for ages."

After coming up through the ranks over the last eleven years, Gavin has had extensive experience working on feature films—one of the reasons why he's so suited to work on the feature-film-quality *Young Indiana Jones Chronicles.* His introduction to Lucasfilm was as an assistant art director on *Return of the Jedi,* where he worked with Norman Reynolds, who, he says, was "instrumental, in a little way, in getting me the job on *The Young Indiana Jones Chronicles.*" In addition, Gavin served as assistant art director on *Superman III, Return to Oz, Young Sherlock Holmes,* and *Supergirl* as well as countless other projects.

As the production designer, it is Gavin's job to bring to life the era in which *The Young Indiana Jones Chronicles* takes place. When watching the series, one is swept away into the early 1900s, giving one the sense of having stepped back in time. For Gavin, the time period we find Young Indy in is something he remembers only from photographs.

To create the authenticity of the time period requires

more than just finding the right location—it also requires finding costumes and vehicles people would have worn and used, too.

"In each country you'll be surprised at what you can find and disappointed in the things you thought you could find but don't. In a city like Prague, Czechoslovakia, they tend to have an awful lot of vehicles—whether or not they're working or you can afford to use them is another story. The people that have vintage cars in Prague are generally quite wealthy people. The city doesn't have film vehicle suppliers, so you find yourself paying an awful lot of money for a day's use of a vehicle."

But these were not the only challenges Gavin faced. Of course, Indiana Jones lives in a specific period of time, but for Gavin, there were sets to design from time periods thousands of years earlier, like the ancient Egyptian tomb from the first two-hour movie. Surprisingly enough, it was not dealing with the grand scale of the pyramids that posed problems for Gavin. Since the episode required many close-ups with characters positioned against Gavin's backdrops, he had to be sure that the finishes and textures looked authentic at close range.

So often in *The Young Indiana Jones Chronicles*, we are caught up in the drama and the action of the story. Much of the time, we don't notice the background or the sets, because they seem as if they are just naturally there. But here, too, a lot of hard work and thought has gone into making those sets accurate. For Gavin Bocquet, the experience of working on the series has been invaluable, not only from a production-design standpoint but also in terms of what he has learned about an exciting time in history.

"I was talking to somebody today about the fact that just from your own educational point of view, you learn all kinds of new things," he says. "You find yourself

saying, 'Oh, I didn't know that.' It shows the quality of
the scripts and their content. . . . I've learned an awful
lot by doing this show."

✪ MAGGIE GRAY
Set Decorator

"I think that I've got the nicest job in the art department," says Maggie Gray, set decorator on *The Young
Indiana Jones Chronicles*. "I think it's the icing on the
cake! I'm given an empty room or location that needs
some kind of interpretation—I literally decorate the
room, from the furniture to the wallpaper and drapes
and right down to the pens, pencils, and ashtrays—every
little personal thing that somebody might be using. I
love my job. It's creating an atmosphere. It's the first
impression you get of a room."

Since they both work on designing the look of the
series' backgrounds and locations, Maggie works very
closely with production designer Gavin Bocquet. They
discuss the look of a room's furnishings and decide on
the color schemes together. "It's teamwork," Maggie
says. "The whole art department works together."

Many of the decorations and furniture you see on *The
Young Indiana Jones Chronicles* are actual antiques that
Maggie finds in a variety of places, from private homes
to large companies that specialize in movie props and
period furniture.

"When I'm in London," she says, "we have a wonderful array of property houses that deal with movies and
the stage. You can walk into some of the prop houses
there and it's like walking into one of the most exquisite
antique shops you've ever seen. There's a wealth of
wonderful things. I also use antique shops in whatever

city we're working in as well as street markets. It's very exciting to find something you've been working very hard to find. We don't normally buy the antiques, we have it on rent. We pay them ten percent of the estimated cost and we have it out for seven days. Then they get it back and they can sell it the next day.

"The nice thing about *The Young Indiana Jones Chronicles*," she continues, "is that there are all different styles for each episode because it takes place in different places around the world."

Our rooms and all the belongings in those rooms reflect something about our personalities. You can tell a lot about a person by examining the way their surroundings look. It is this idea that helps reveal further aspects of the characters on *The Young Indiana Jones Chronicles*. One example of this is the way Helen Seymour's house was decorated in the London episode. Because she lives on her own and is an educator, Maggie decided that Helen should have a lot of interesting leatherbound books around. She's looked after her furniture very well, and because she lives alone, she isn't very organized. Of course, in her travels all over the world as Indy's tutor, she has found all kinds of little trinkets. Naturally, Maggie tried to display some of these throughout her home. "I enjoyed doing her house a lot," says Maggie. "I had an affinity with her."

Traveling from country to country and searching in various cities for furniture and props can be a very time-consuming and tiring task. With only two weeks to shoot each episode, Maggie is always working with the restriction of time.

"We're working very, very fast," she says. "I found it a strain at the beginning to actually keep up and to give every set as much time as I wanted to give it. Also, when we started shooting, we weren't doing one complete episode. We would have a week where we were doing a part of Spain, then a part of China, and then a section in London. I had to keep switching myself to different countries although I was based in London. My one regret is that we haven't had more time to work on everything."

Despite this frustration Maggie is quick to add, "The nice thing about my job is that it's so versatile. One minute I'm doing a grand ballroom, and then the next minute I'm down in the bunker room somewhere underground or out in the trenches. And the next day I'm in a Russian café. It's incredibly varied. It's been a wonderful experience even though I've had to work very fast!"

6

Filming All Over the World

With fifteen episodes being shot literally all over the world and on an extremely limited budget, *The Young Indiana Jones Chronicles* is indeed one of the most ambitious projects in television history. It is a classic in the making. But each country poses unique problems for the production crew—everything from language barriers to concerns with transportation, food, shelter, foreign money exchange, and crowd control, just to name a few. For executive producer George Lucas and producer Rick McCallum, organization and planning are a must in order for each episode to be completed on time. But unfortunately, some things just can't be planned for, such as sickness or accidents, both of which have struck the *Young Indiana Jones* cast and crew. But for every problem there is a solution. True teamwork was needed to deal with all that McCallum describes here.

"In Africa, we actually built a village in the middle of the Tana River," he states. "There is absolutely no civilization nearby, it's virtually in the jungle. We literally had to create a whole city. We had to create our own water sanitation plants, our own toilets, and everybody lived in tents for about eight weeks. We had to build our own roads, set up an efficient system for bringing in materials, we had to build a landing strip, docks for boats, and dams to prevent flooding from where we were. We had to set up a base camp, construction mill, and bring in electricity. We also had many problems with illness because it's very hard to treat the water because of the volume. It was very, very hot and everybody was drinking about six or seven pints a day. When you get a local crew of about sixty people together, then add our basic, small crew of about twenty-five, it becomes a small village. Plus I had children and animals and we were very close to the Somalia border, so we had to set up a security force with trenches and barbed wire because we had weapons. So that was quite an experience. About twelve people got seriously ill, a boat hit a sandbar and capsized on a very dangerous curve of the Tana River where there are usually fourteen or fifteen crocodiles. So it's been an unusual experience."

The first episode of the *Chronicles* has us following Indy at age eighteen to London, England, where he meets the love of his life, Vicky Prentiss. England is the home of most of the production crew, including McCallum. Not surprisingly, this is where they feel the most comfortable, so shooting there wasn't as difficult as it was in other places. Some of the scenes in the China episode and interiors from the Egyptian episode were shot in England as well.

From England we travel to Spain. Barcelona is one of the most beautiful cities in Spain, and it's the location for the Spanish episode directed by Terry Jones. Many of the cast and crew have fond memories of the time they spent in this wonderful city, including Indy himself, Sean Patrick Flanery.

"It was the only place that we've been that was actually

populated by people I could communicate with," the young actor says with a smile. "We'd go to Africa, and the whole culture's completely different. Even if you could communicate—even if we did speak the same language—they have no knowledge of electricity. You can't just get into a conversation for hours with those people. We were in Prague, where people stand in line for eight hours to get a four-ounce piece of beef, and we're on the set with ample food. The culture is so different. Communication is almost impossible. We have translators there, but it was still difficult. Finally, we got to Spain, and it was, like, real . . . the kind of people for whom going out to eat at night is not a heart-stopping event! So I really liked Spain. There were things to do on your time off, and I loved it. There were beaches, and the sun was out. Everybody was smiling and happy."

Next stop on our *Young Indiana Jones* tour of the world is the exotic country of China—home to almost 1.3 billion people. It is here that the eight-year-old Indy sees the Great Wall of China, completed in the third century B.C. and stretching over two thousand miles.

"China is basically the same size as America," says McCallum, "but with six times as many people. There is no place you can go where there isn't the most extraordinary amount of people. Yesterday, when we were shooting on the street, there were almost ten thousand people standing by watching us. It creates great problems. You cannot get enough assistance to move the traffic. There is not enough security, nor enough willpower to get that many people to move. But, again, we had a wonderful Chinese crew. It was the very first time they ever worked on a Western film. They're learning enormously and it is an extraordinary country. It's extraordinary in the sense that most of us forget about how lucky we are with what we have. We also forget what an extraordinary state of near survival everybody else in this world lives in. For instance, in Africa, just this year alone, over fourteen million people have died of starvation."

Nearly all of the *Young Indiana Jones Chronicles* cast and crew speak about their incredible experience in Africa. It is a country practically untouched by time. It is home to some of the most wild and beautiful creatures on the planet Earth, and it was the home of the earliest, primitive man—a perfect place to film an Indiana Jones adventure.

"Africa was *the* most powerful experience yet," says McCallum. "We got to shoot in the Maasai Mora and in the Tana River. There were the most extraordinary people there. There is just something that reaches very deep inside you that you tap into. There's just something about—not just the animal kingdom, but this unique balance of life that is absolutely perfection. It is an extraordinary continent. Once you get out of Nairobi, Kenya, life has not changed for a thousand years. It's incredible."

"I loved Africa," agrees Sean Patrick Flanery. "We stayed in Lamu. It was in an actual hotel, but there's no glass-plate windows. There are just these holes in the side of the room where you could see the ocean. It was gorgeous—white sand, sun coming up every morning. It was a gorgeous place, but a filthy city. Our hotel was the only hotel on the entire island. The other ones are just guest houses—no electricity, no windows or anything, and there are huge spiders that would cruise in my window—diameter probably four and a half, five inches—huge, furry spiders, and there was this little can of this 'kills-it' spray sitting on the shelf that comes with a surgical mask. On the directions it says in English, 'Hold six feet away from insect you intend to kill, turn your face away, wear a gas mask, and leave the premises immediately after firing if possible.' This is toxic stuff that you can't get in the States! I zapped these things from six feet away, and they froze in their tracks, just like you shellacked them on the wall. I mean, they were frozen. They wouldn't move. It was bizarre!"

Out of all the locations the *Chronicles* crew was shooting, Prague, Czechoslovakia, is where they spent the most time—nearly seventeen weeks. And the one word Rick McCallum would use to describe their stay in this beautiful, historic city is "cold." In fact, the climate is the exact opposite of Africa.

"Prague is probably the last great European capital left intact," the producer states. "It also has a very fine and sophisticated film community. It's going through an enormous change right now from communism to capitalism, which is extremely difficult. They have huge inflation—forty percent this year. These are very, very tough times for a lot of people, especially the people in their late forties or early fifties and older. Suddenly their whole life is being switched around on them. So that's causing enormous cultural problems and financial problems.

"Prague virtually has four square miles that have not been touched for almost four hundred years," the producer maintains. "In fact, a year ago, the city actually began to help us and ripped up some of the streets and put back some of the original cobblestones. They did it for us because they knew we needed the square, but they also did it as an overall plan to return the city back to its early 1910 state. So we have the original gas lamps, all the cobblestone streets, and the huge squares where no automobiles are allowed to go. Prague has been the easiest to film in because of that."

Another country going through major changes is the

While filming all over the world, the series makeup artists, set designers, and actors took their cues from many of the natives.

Soviet Union. At the time of this writing the cast and crew had not yet made the journey to Russia, where they would be shooting an episode with Indy as he witnesses the Russian Revolution. As is the case in other economically struggling countries, the Soviet people sometimes have to wait in line seven or eight hours a day for food and the basic essentials just to make it through a single day. "I've never seen such real chaos and real deep-down hunger and despair," says McCallum. "We were actually going to shoot sooner in Russia, but it became very apparent to us that during the summer it was going to be very tricky because there was a lot of stuff going on. We were lucky that we weren't there during the coup."

One of the most enchanting countries the crew visited was Austria, located right next door to Czechoslovakia. Based in Vienna, the capital, the crew had only days to enjoy this beautiful city on the Danube River.

The strange and mystical country of India is where Indy's adventures take him as a young boy, long before his adventure in *The Temple of Doom*. It is here that he is introduced to the young philosopher Krishnamurti. But shooting in India was not an easy task.

"Benares, the holy city in India, was very difficult to get approval to shoot in," says McCallum. "It took us nine months, but we basically got carte blanche and we can now shoot everywhere we need to."

Of course, our journey of the world with Young Indy would not be complete without a stop in the romantic city of Paris, France. It is here that our hero meets up with some of the greatest artists of all time—Picasso, Degas, and a young Norman Rockwell. "I love the city— it's one of the great places to visit, to be in, and to have a good time in, but it is a very, very difficult city to film in," notes McCallum.

The last stop on our travels is the ancient land of Egypt. With its great pyramids stretching to the sky, Egypt is probably the country most people would associate with an Indiana Jones adventure, but while it does have a certain magic touch, shooting there was far from perfect.

"That was the only true nightmare that I've had so far," McCallum admits. "I had a wonderful Egyptian crew, but you cannot understand certain countries like India, China, Russia, and all of the Middle East until you understand the bureaucracies there and how people are controlled. The bureaucracy in Egypt is mind numbing. There are ten people to do a job that, in any other country, one person would be doing. Where we were shooting it was virtually a hundred and forty degrees every day in the middle of the desert. It was very difficult to get water supplies in where we were. Food was almost inedible. It was, without question, the most difficult location we've had so far. The heat was extraordinary. We lost more Egyptians than we did our crew. They're not used to working throughout the day. They are very sensible, they take a siesta during the day.

"Egypt was so hard to shoot in partially because of the heat and partially because everything we needed to shoot has almost been destroyed," McCallum continues. "They didn't want me to show the pyramids, they wanted me to show the power lines that stretch all around the pyramids. When I was in Aswan, they didn't want me to show people washing their clothes in the river, they wanted me to show the new hospital, because all of those things, those relics of an ancient era, are repugnant to them. They are trying to survive now and show they are making huge efforts in education and health care. It's a big conceptual way of looking at life, and those relics are meaningless to them at this time.

It's the same way in China—they're much more interested in surviving.

"One of the ways that we have promoted good relations is that we don't live any differently than the people in the country we're filming in. That's what usually causes the greatest problems," says McCallum. "Once you go into a country and try to impose your will on the group of people you're actually working with, they get angry. They have their pride. They want to learn the best of what we have, but they also want to maintain their own dignity. In China, money is not important; nor was it in Egypt. You can't buy your way through with things. It's all about saving face and being honorable, but certainly the most important thing, especially in a communist state like China, is that everyone has to be treated the same. Basically, we live like the people in the country we visit. And that's certainly been helpful in Africa, China, and Egypt."

While the different cultures that McCallum and crew encounter in each country pose problems for them, it's nothing they can't overcome. When you've traveled around the world, you begin to realize the incredible diversity of people and their different ways of living. The life-style in China is vastly different from the life-style in Spain—everything from language to clothing and even food. And growing accustomed to the different foreign cuisines is something the cast and crew have had to face and have grown to enjoy.

"Spain has had the best food so far," says McCallum. "But Africa was extremely tough because we had a lot of salmonella poisoning, which resulted in a lot of very sick people. We had diarrhea and stomach cramps. Czechoslovakia was very tough, too. The food is very heavy and there isn't a lot of choice. Vegetables are very rare. We actually had to send a truck to Germany once a week to load up on vegetables because we were getting vitamin deficiencies and gum disease. It's amazing how sensitive and how spoiled Western stomachs are compared with the rest of the world. You know, you don't get fine-grained rice in China: it's got rocks and bits of earth in it. China has been very difficult because they eat a full Chinese meal at breakfast, like what we eat at dinner, and that's been tough on the crew. Their meat is not processed in any way, so it has an odor about it that a lot of English and American people find extremely difficult to handle. Most tourists that go to China stay at the Hilton. They can virtually have hot dogs and hamburgers and pizza there. But we don't have anything to do with any of that because the minute we embark on that route, we have shifted that whole balance we have with every crew we're working with. It means then that we're actually living another life, and to many of them, that means living a lie, where we say one thing and do another."

Moving the cast and crew from country to country is like moving an army. It takes months of preparation and planning. There are plane tickets to book, transportation in the specific countries to arrange, hotel rooms to reserve, caterers to be contacted—all of which are things Rick McCallum must organize before the cast and crew arrive in the country in which they are shooting.

"There are enormous customs problems because I bring maybe twenty thousand pounds of equipment—all our camera equipment, wardrobe, the props. The visas take up to ninety days before we can get them, the casting of talent in different cities has to be brought all together, the food arrangements are crucial because when you're shooting in China, you just can't go to McDonald's for lunch. In half the places we've been there haven't been restaurants for miles. The water and sanitation services have to be arranged. People have to go to the bathroom in a bowl sometimes because there aren't bathrooms. In Africa, everybody lived in tents and there was water boiled once a day and hung from a tree, just a regular water bucket, and that's how everybody took their showers. It's a great deal of work, but I wouldn't trade it for anything in the world.

"You know, I love to travel and visiting these different countries has given me a real education," concludes McCallum. "I've done one hundred and seventy-five thousand miles this year. I've traveled all over the world and I consider myself a very fortunate man to be involved with George Lucas and *The Young Indiana Jones Chronicles*."

7

A Visit to the Set of *The Young Indiana Jones Chronicles*

What is it like to spend a day on the set of *The Young Indiana Jones Chronicles*? On any particular day, if you were to visit, you would find a busy group of people working feverishly to ensure that everything—the cameras, the sets, the actors, the costumes, the lights, the makeup, the sound equipment, the props, etc.—is ready to go.

On one particular day we found the cast and crew setting up a shot inside an open tent for the British East Africa 1909 episode. Inside the tent are cages filled with a variety of small birds and monkeys. Tables are set up with what appear to be skinned animals that they have just brought in from Roosevelt's African hunt (they're not real animals, however, but extremely good replicas of a zebra, a lion, and a gazelle). The set looks as if we had just stepped back in time to an African safari in 1909.

All around us people are rushing to add last-minute touches. The director and his crew are practicing the tracking shot with the camera. (A tracking shot is a shot in which the camera moves on tracks to film a moving subject.) In this case Young Indy and an old friend of his father's, Richard Medlicot, are to be filmed as they enter the tent. The director and his crew set up the camera outside of the tent. Inside, crew people are making sure all the props—everything from tables and chairs to bird cages and elephant tusks—are sitting in their proper place. Over in the corner the script supervisor reads through the pages of the script one more time to make sure the actors say the right lines. Sometimes they can slip up, so it's important that the script supervisor be familiar with the dialogue and that a script is available right in front of him or her to read as the actors say their lines.

Down on the floor, under the table, is the sound man. He is holding a large sound mike to make sure the actors' words are heard loud and clear on film. Many times the actors' words do not come through clearly, and months later, after shooting has been completed, the actors have to go to a recording studio to repeat their lines. This process is called "dubbing."

As the director and the cinematographer peer through the camera lens to make sure the shot is focused correctly, the actors Corey Carrier and Edward Tudor-Pole rehearse their lines and movements in front of them. It's not only important that they repeat their lines properly, but that they also move with the camera and stand in the proper places. They may rehearse one scene several times to make sure it works right. After three or four rehearsals the director shouts to the crew for quiet, and then yells, "Action!" As Corey and the other actor begin to walk side by side, the camera moves down the track following them. The two actors enter the tent and meet the other actor in the scene, who is playing a character named Heller. Heller is a taxidermist from the Smithsonian Institute, who skins the dead animals so they can be taken back to the United States. His hands are messy with blood from the animals (keep in mind that everything is fake—the blood, the dead animals, etc.). After a few seconds of looking around the tent, the dialogue begins:

RICHARD: Heller! let me introduce you to Henry Jones, Jr., Professor Jones's son.
INDY: Pleased to meet you, Mr. Heller.

Heller holds out a bloodstained hand and Indy shakes it, then sees the blood.

RICHARD: Heller's from the Smithsonian. He's a taxidermist, he prepares the specimens for transportation back to the United States.
HELLER: One of the less glamorous jobs, but nonetheless the reason we're here—you see, Henry, this is a scientific expedition. The next time you go into a museum and stare at a lion, you can think of me and my bloodstained hands.

The director yells, "Cut," and the scene ends. He seems pleased with the way everything went and decides to keep it and move on to the next scene. Immediately the crew begins moving about, setting up all the elements for the next scene to shoot. Some of the actors walk back to their chairs under a nice cool tent. There they will wait until the next shot is ready for them. One actor, however, has found something interesting to occupy his time. Corey Carrier has wandered off and found the man who handles the animals on the set. One creature in particular has sparked Corey's curiosity. In the young actor's hands is a baby snake—a boa constrictor—and Corey shows no signs of fear. The snake begins to crawl around his neck as he giggles. He looks the snake straight in the face and remarks that he would like to have one for a pet. Several other children wander over and begin to look at the snake. Corey proudly shows them that the snake is harmless as the other children watch in awe.

Over on the other side of the tent the actors that portray Indy's mother and father are heavy in discussion with several crew people. They're talking about the upcoming scene. A wardrobe person checks actress Ruth De Sosa's dress to make sure it fits properly. A makeup person walks up and puts the finishing touches on their makeup—they don't need much, just a little to keep the glare off their faces. Inside the tent a crew person in charge of the live animals checks the birds and feeds the monkeys. The crew makes sure that the animals are treated well and that they are not abused. Lucasfilm has made a conscious effort on *The Young Indiana Jones Chronicles* to see that all of the animals used in the series are well taken care of.

As the camera crew sets up for the next shot, the lighting crew talks with the director about what kind of lighting he wants for the scene. Although they are shooting outdoors, there is still a certain amount of artificial lighting required to remove shadows and, generally, create enough light on the actors' faces. There seems to be plenty of light, though, as it is a very hot, sunny day on the African grasslands. Many native people, who have been hired to work on the production, are busy at their particular jobs and seem to be impressed with the size and scope of this production. It's not every day that a production like *The Young Indiana Jones Chronicles* comes to their part of the world. Many of them are conversing in their native African tongue as they smile and go about their work.

There is a familiar hubbub as the cast and crew all work together to film each episode of the series. Whether they're in Spain, Egypt, Czechoslovakia, or Africa, the work is the same—the locations just change. Each individual has his or her area of expertise and works long, hard hours with the others to perfect what we see on our television screens each week.

While we've given you a glimpse of what goes into the making of *The Young Indiana Jones Chronicles,* we should emphasize that this is a work in progress. At the writing of this book some of the cast and crew were in Prague, Czechoslovakia, shooting several episodes, while other cast and crew members, along with producer Rick McCallum, were in China shooting at the Great Wall. Many of the episodes hadn't been filmed yet, so, certainly, some things were left out. But even at this stage it appears as if George Lucas has created a timeless television series that does more than chronicle the youth of Indiana Jones. This series entertains us by sharing the same sense of adventure and mystery that first brought us into the movie theaters to see the daring archaeologist with the fedora hat and the trusty bullwhip at his side. But *The Young Indiana Jones Chronicles* also shares history with us—the deeply personal history of one boy as he matures into a man of action and integrity, as well as a broader history which we all share as inhabitants of this world. Besides telling us some great stories, this show satisfies our yearning to experience the things that are the most exciting, rich, and rewarding in life. Though young in years, Indiana Jones has had some thrilling experiences and he's invited us all to come along for the ride of his life!

T·H·E LUCASFILM FAN CLUB

NEW

Follow the adventures of Young Indiana Jones through the pages of the Official Lucasfilm Fan Club Magazine! Each issue has exclusive features, beautiful full-color photos, behind-the-scenes articles, and interviews with the people who make *The Young Indiana Jones Chronicles*. Plus there are features on other Lucasfilm projects like *Star Wars* and *Willow* and on the Disney theme-park spectaculars, Lucasfilm Games and Industrial Light and Magic— the special effects wizards! You can also purchase genuine collectors items through the club's official merchandise catalog such as posters, toys, books, and clothing as well as products made exclusively for members only!

YOUR MEMBERSHIP INCLUDES:
A fantastic Young Indiana Jones Chronicles Membership Kit including a beautiful full-color poster, photos, welcome letter from George Lucas, membership card and much, much more!

PLUS:
• One-year subscription to the quarterly full-color Lucasfilm Magazine!
• Cast and crew fan mail forwarding!
• Classified section!

JOIN FOR ONLY $9.95